The Cup of Coffee

A Hidden in Plain View Series
by Melly Nofal and Lourdes Welhaven

ISBN-13: 978-1511769211

ISBN-10: 1511769211

Cover and page design by Welhaven and Associates.

For more information on this and other similar titles go to www.hiddeninplainviewbooks.com

THE CUP OF COFFEE

The Secretive Password Organizer Log That's Hidden in Plain View.

Seems like there's a password required for everything these days. Can't remember them all? No more worries! Keep all your important password information organized and easily accessible in one place in this convenient and unique password organizer logbook.

"The Cup of Coffee" is a Password Organizer Log unlike any other. It does not announce to the world: "Hey! I'm an important password book!" Instead, it looks like a regular book. The goal in the layout of "The Cup of Coffee" is to provide an extra layer of secrecy to your password information. We intentionally designed it to look like a novel from the outside. This design is based on the premise that the very best hiding place is in plain view. This way, anyone casually glancing at your password book will have no clue that it contains your important and valuable passwords. You're the only one who needs to know that.

"The Cup of Coffee" is laid out in a simple and easy-to-use format providing quick access to your passwords when you need them. It contains 100 pages with spots for 200 entries for storing all of your internet sites and accounts. It is fully customizable. With 2 entry spots per page, you have ample room to list your personal passwords, usernames, password hints, PINs, security questions, as well as additional notes for each. In addition, the space at the top right corner of each page is left blank so that you can alphabetize the pages yourself, according to your needs, since you may require more entries under one letter than another.

Keep your information safe in "The Cup of Coffee" and never worry about forgetting or misplacing vital password information written all over the place ever again. With a cover that looks like a regular book and a comfortable size of 5" x 8", "The Cup of Coffee" is the perfect organizational tool to make your life easier and also to give as a gift to others. Check out our website for other innovative ideas at www.hiddeninplainviewbooks.com.

Disclaimer: Please be aware that your password and other information that you put into "The Cup of Coffee" is extremely important. Guard and protect it carefully as you do not want it to get into the wrong hands. Remember – it is up to YOU, and you alone, to keep it safe and secure. By using this book, you acknowledge and agree that you are solely responsible for the security of the information entered into the book. You further acknowledge and agree that neither "The Cup of Coffee" password organizer log nor the authors are liable in any way for any damages resulting from the theft, loss or unauthorized use of your book and/or the information you placed inside it.

Starting with the Letter(s) A,B,C

Name _Amazon_

Website _____ www.Amazon.com

User Name _____ you@mail.com

Password _____ 123LetMeIn

Password Hint _____

PIN _____

Security Questions/Notes _I love Prime Membership!_

Changed password on 1-2-14

_____

_____

Above is an Example Entry

This page intentionally left blank.

Starting with the Letter(s)

Name _____

Website _____

User Name _____

Password _____

Password Hint _____

PIN _____

Security Questions/Notes _____

_____

_____

_____

Name _____

Website _____

User Name _____

Password _____

Password Hint _____

PIN _____

Security Questions/Notes _____

_____

_____

_____

Starting with the Letter(s)

Name

Website

User Name

Password

Password Hint

PIN

Security Questions/Notes

Name

Website

User Name

Password

Password Hint

PIN

Security Questions/Notes

Starting with the Letter(s)

Name _____

Website _____

User Name _____

Password _____

Password Hint _____

PIN _____

Security Questions/Notes_____

_____

_____

_____

Name _____

Website _____

User Name _____

Password _____

Password Hint _____

PIN _____

Security Questions/Notes_____

_____

_____

_____

Starting with the Letter(s)

Name

Website _____

User Name _____

Password _____

Password Hint _____

PIN _____

Security Questions/Notes_____

_____

_____

_____

Name

Website _____

User Name _____

Password _____

Password Hint _____

PIN _____

Security Questions/Notes_____

_____

_____

_____

Starting with the Letter(s)

Name _____

Website _____

User Name _____

Password _____

Password Hint _____

PIN _____

Security Questions/Notes_____

_____

_____

_____

Name _____

Website _____

User Name _____

Password _____

Password Hint _____

PIN _____

Security Questions/Notes_____

_____

_____

_____

Starting with the Letter(s)

Name _____

Website _____

User Name _____

Password _____

Password Hint _____

PIN _____

Security Questions/Notes _____

_____

_____

_____

Name _____

Website _____

User Name _____

Password _____

Password Hint _____

PIN _____

Security Questions/Notes _____

_____

_____

_____

Starting with the Letter(s)

Name _____

Website _____

User Name _____

Password _____

Password Hint _____

PIN _____

Security Questions/Notes_____

_____

_____

_____

Name _____

Website _____

User Name _____

Password _____

Password Hint _____

PIN _____

Security Questions/Notes_____

_____

_____

_____

Starting with the Letter(s)

Name _____

Website _____

User Name _____

Password _____

Password Hint _____

PIN _____

Security Questions/Notes_____

_____

_____

_____

Name _____

Website _____

User Name _____

Password _____

Password Hint _____

PIN _____

Security Questions/Notes_____

_____

_____

_____

Starting with the Letter(s)

Name _____

Website _____

User Name _____

Password _____

Password Hint _____

PIN _____

Security Questions/Notes_____

_____

_____

_____

Name _____

Website _____

User Name _____

Password _____

Password Hint _____

PIN _____

Security Questions/Notes_____

_____

_____

_____

Starting with the Letter(s)

Name

Website ———————————————————

User Name ———————————————————

Password ———————————————————

Password Hint ———————————————————

PIN ———————————————————

Security Questions/Notes———————————————

———————————————————

———————————————————

———————————————————

Name

Website ———————————————————

User Name ———————————————————

Password ———————————————————

Password Hint ———————————————————

PIN ———————————————————

Security Questions/Notes———————————————

———————————————————

———————————————————

———————————————————

Starting with the Letter(s)

Name _____

Website _____

User Name _____

Password _____

Password Hint _____

PIN _____

Security Questions/Notes _____

_____

_____

_____

Name _____

Website _____

User Name _____

Password _____

Password Hint _____

PIN _____

Security Questions/Notes _____

_____

_____

_____

Starting with the Letter(s)

Name _____

Website _____

User Name _____

Password _____

Password Hint _____

PIN _____

Security Questions/Notes_____

_____

_____

_____

Name _____

Website _____

User Name _____

Password _____

Password Hint _____

PIN _____

Security Questions/Notes_____

_____

_____

_____

Starting with the Letter(s)

Name _____

Website _____

User Name _____

Password _____

Password Hint _____

PIN _____

Security Questions/Notes_____

_____

_____

_____

Name _____

Website _____

User Name _____

Password _____

Password Hint _____

PIN _____

Security Questions/Notes_____

_____

_____

_____

Starting with the Letter(s)

Name _____

Website _____

User Name _____

Password _____

Password Hint _____

PIN _____

Security Questions/Notes _____

_____

_____

_____

Name _____

Website _____

User Name _____

Password _____

Password Hint _____

PIN _____

Security Questions/Notes _____

_____

_____

_____

Starting with the Letter(s)

Name _____

Website _____

User Name _____

Password _____

Password Hint _____

PIN _____

Security Questions/Notes _____

_____

_____

_____

Name _____

Website _____

User Name _____

Password _____

Password Hint _____

PIN _____

Security Questions/Notes _____

_____

_____

_____

Starting with the Letter(s)

Name _____

Website _____

User Name _____

Password _____

Password Hint _____

PIN _____

Security Questions/Notes_____

_____

_____

_____

Name _____

Website _____

User Name _____

Password _____

Password Hint _____

PIN _____

Security Questions/Notes_____

_____

_____

_____

Starting with the Letter(s)

Name _____

Website _____

User Name _____

Password _____

Password Hint _____

PIN _____

Security Questions/Notes _____

_____

_____

_____

Name _____

Website _____

User Name _____

Password _____

Password Hint _____

PIN _____

Security Questions/Notes _____

_____

_____

_____

Starting with the Letter(s)

Name

Website

User Name

Password

Password Hint

PIN

Security Questions/Notes

Name

Website

User Name

Password

Password Hint

PIN

Security Questions/Notes

Starting with the Letter(s)

Name _____

Website _____

User Name _____

Password _____

Password Hint _____

PIN _____

Security Questions/Notes_____

_____

_____

_____

Name _____

Website _____

User Name _____

Password _____

Password Hint _____

PIN _____

Security Questions/Notes_____

_____

_____

_____

Starting with the Letter(s)

Name _____

Website _____

User Name _____

Password _____

Password Hint _____

PIN _____

Security Questions/Notes_____

_____

_____

_____

Name _____

Website _____

User Name _____

Password _____

Password Hint _____

PIN _____

Security Questions/Notes_____

_____

_____

_____

Starting with the Letter(s)

Name _____

Website _____

User Name _____

Password _____

Password Hint _____

PIN _____

Security Questions/Notes_____

_____

_____

_____

Name _____

Website _____

User Name _____

Password _____

Password Hint _____

PIN _____

Security Questions/Notes_____

_____

_____

_____

Starting with the Letter(s)

Name _____

Website _____

User Name _____

Password _____

Password Hint _____

PIN _____

Security Questions/Notes_____

_____

_____

_____

Name _____

Website _____

User Name _____

Password _____

Password Hint _____

PIN _____

Security Questions/Notes_____

_____

_____

_____

Starting with the Letter(s)

Name _____

Website _____

User Name _____

Password _____

Password Hint _____

PIN _____

Security Questions/Notes_____

_____

_____

_____

Name _____

Website _____

User Name _____

Password _____

Password Hint _____

PIN _____

Security Questions/Notes_____

_____

_____

_____

Starting with the Letter(s)

Name _____

Website _____

User Name _____

Password _____

Password Hint _____

PIN _____

Security Questions/Notes_____

_____

_____

_____

Name _____

Website _____

User Name _____

Password _____

Password Hint _____

PIN _____

Security Questions/Notes_____

_____

_____

_____

Starting with the Letter(s)

Name _____

Website _____

User Name _____

Password _____

Password Hint _____

PIN _____

Security Questions/Notes_____

_____

_____

_____

Name _____

Website _____

User Name _____

Password _____

Password Hint _____

PIN _____

Security Questions/Notes_____

_____

_____

_____

Starting with the Letter(s)

Name

Website

User Name

Password

Password Hint

PIN

Security Questions/Notes

Name

Website

User Name

Password

Password Hint

PIN

Security Questions/Notes

Name _____

Website _____

User Name _____

Password _____

Password Hint _____

PIN _____

Security Questions/Notes_____

_____

_____

_____

Name _____

Website _____

User Name _____

Password _____

Password Hint _____

PIN _____

Security Questions/Notes_____

_____

_____

_____

Starting with the Letter(s)

Name _____

Website _____

User Name _____

Password _____

Password Hint _____

PIN _____

Security Questions/Notes_____

_____

_____

_____

Name _____

Website _____

User Name _____

Password _____

Password Hint _____

PIN _____

Security Questions/Notes_____

_____

_____

_____

Starting with the Letter(s)

Name _____

Website _____

User Name _____

Password _____

Password Hint _____

PIN _____

Security Questions/Notes_____

_____

_____

_____

Name _____

Website _____

User Name _____

Password _____

Password Hint _____

PIN _____

Security Questions/Notes_____

_____

_____

_____

Starting with the Letter(s)

Name _____

Website _____

User Name _____

Password _____

Password Hint _____

PIN _____

Security Questions/Notes_____

_____

_____

_____

Name _____

Website _____

User Name _____

Password _____

Password Hint _____

PIN _____

Security Questions/Notes_____

_____

_____

_____

Starting with the Letter(s)

Name _____

Website _____

User Name _____

Password _____

Password Hint _____

PIN _____

Security Questions/Notes _____

_____

_____

_____

Name _____

Website _____

User Name _____

Password _____

Password Hint _____

PIN _____

Security Questions/Notes _____

_____

_____

_____

Starting with the Letter(s)

Name _____

Website _____

User Name _____

Password _____

Password Hint _____

PIN _____

Security Questions/Notes_____

_____

_____

_____

Name _____

Website _____

User Name _____

Password _____

Password Hint _____

PIN _____

Security Questions/Notes_____

_____

_____

_____

Starting with the Letter(s)

Name _____

Website _____

User Name _____

Password _____

Password Hint _____

PIN _____

Security Questions/Notes_____

_____

_____

_____

Name _____

Website _____

User Name _____

Password _____

Password Hint _____

PIN _____

Security Questions/Notes_____

_____

_____

_____

Starting with the Letter(s)

Name _____

Website _____

User Name _____

Password _____

Password Hint _____

PIN _____

Security Questions/Notes_____

_____

_____

_____

Name _____

Website _____

User Name _____

Password _____

Password Hint _____

PIN _____

Security Questions/Notes_____

_____

_____

_____

Starting with the Letter(s)

Name _____

Website _____

User Name _____

Password _____

Password Hint _____

PIN _____

Security Questions/Notes_____

_____

_____

_____

Name _____

Website _____

User Name _____

Password _____

Password Hint _____

PIN _____

Security Questions/Notes_____

_____

_____

_____

Starting with the Letter(s)

Name _____

Website _____

User Name _____

Password _____

Password Hint _____

PIN _____

Security Questions/Notes_____

_____

_____

_____

Name _____

Website _____

User Name _____

Password _____

Password Hint _____

PIN _____

Security Questions/Notes_____

_____

_____

_____

Starting with the Letter(s)

Name _____

Website _____

User Name _____

Password _____

Password Hint _____

PIN _____

Security Questions/Notes_____

_____

_____

_____

Name _____

Website _____

User Name _____

Password _____

Password Hint _____

PIN _____

Security Questions/Notes_____

_____

_____

_____

Starting with the Letter(s)

Name _____

Website _____

User Name _____

Password _____

Password Hint _____

PIN _____

Security Questions/Notes_____

_____

_____

_____

Name _____

Website _____

User Name _____

Password _____

Password Hint _____

PIN _____

Security Questions/Notes_____

_____

_____

_____

Starting with the Letter(s)

Name _____

Website _____

User Name _____

Password _____

Password Hint _____

PIN _____

Security Questions/Notes_____

_____

_____

_____

Name _____

Website _____

User Name _____

Password _____

Password Hint _____

PIN _____

Security Questions/Notes_____

_____

_____

_____

Starting with the Letter(s)

Name _____

Website _____

User Name _____

Password _____

Password Hint _____

PIN _____

Security Questions/Notes _____

_____

_____

_____

Name _____

Website _____

User Name _____

Password _____

Password Hint _____

PIN _____

Security Questions/Notes _____

_____

_____

_____

Starting with the Letter(s)

Name _____

Website _____

User Name _____

Password _____

Password Hint _____

PIN _____

Security Questions/Notes_____

_____

_____

_____

Name _____

Website _____

User Name _____

Password _____

Password Hint _____

PIN _____

Security Questions/Notes_____

_____

_____

_____

Starting with the Letter(s)

Name _____

Website _____

User Name _____

Password _____

Password Hint _____

PIN _____

Security Questions/Notes _____

_____

_____

_____

Name _____

Website _____

User Name _____

Password _____

Password Hint _____

PIN _____

Security Questions/Notes _____

_____

_____

_____

Starting with the Letter(s)

Name _____

Website _____

User Name _____

Password _____

Password Hint _____

PIN _____

Security Questions/Notes_____

_____

_____

_____

Name _____

Website _____

User Name _____

Password _____

Password Hint _____

PIN _____

Security Questions/Notes_____

_____

_____

_____

Starting with the Letter(s)

Name _____

Website _____

User Name _____

Password _____

Password Hint _____

PIN _____

Security Questions/Notes_____

_____

_____

_____

Name _____

Website _____

User Name _____

Password _____

Password Hint _____

PIN _____

Security Questions/Notes_____

_____

_____

_____

Starting with the Letter(s)

Name _____

Website _____

User Name _____

Password _____

Password Hint _____

PIN _____

Security Questions/Notes_____

_____

_____

_____

Name _____

Website _____

User Name _____

Password _____

Password Hint _____

PIN _____

Security Questions/Notes_____

_____

_____

_____

Starting with the Letter(s)

Name _____

Website _____

User Name _____

Password _____

Password Hint _____

PIN _____

Security Questions/Notes_____

_____

_____

_____

Name _____

Website _____

User Name _____

Password _____

Password Hint _____

PIN _____

Security Questions/Notes_____

_____

_____

_____

Starting with the Letter(s)

Name _____

Website _____

User Name _____

Password _____

Password Hint _____

PIN _____

Security Questions/Notes_____

_____

_____

_____

Name _____

Website _____

User Name _____

Password _____

Password Hint _____

PIN _____

Security Questions/Notes_____

_____

_____

_____

Starting with the Letter(s)

Name _____

Website _____

User Name _____

Password _____

Password Hint _____

PIN _____

Security Questions/Notes_____

_____

_____

_____

Name _____

Website _____

User Name _____

Password _____

Password Hint _____

PIN _____

Security Questions/Notes_____

_____

_____

_____

Starting with the Letter(s)

Name

Website

User Name

Password

Password Hint

PIN

Security Questions/Notes

Name

Website

User Name

Password

Password Hint

PIN

Security Questions/Notes

Starting with the Letter(s)

Name

Website

User Name

Password

Password Hint

PIN

Security Questions/Notes

Name

Website

User Name

Password

Password Hint

PIN

Security Questions/Notes

Starting with the Letter(s)

Name _____

Website _____

User Name _____

Password _____

Password Hint _____

PIN _____

Security Questions/Notes_____

_____

_____

_____

Name _____

Website _____

User Name _____

Password _____

Password Hint _____

PIN _____

Security Questions/Notes_____

_____

_____

_____

Starting with the Letter(s)

Name _____

Website _____

User Name _____

Password _____

Password Hint _____

PIN _____

Security Questions/Notes_____

_____

_____

_____

Name _____

Website _____

User Name _____

Password _____

Password Hint _____

PIN _____

Security Questions/Notes_____

_____

_____

_____

Starting with the Letter(s)

Name _____

Website _____

User Name _____

Password _____

Password Hint _____

PIN _____

Security Questions/Notes_____

_____

_____

_____

Name _____

Website _____

User Name _____

Password _____

Password Hint _____

PIN _____

Security Questions/Notes_____

_____

_____

_____

Starting with the Letter(s)

Name _____

Website _____

User Name _____

Password _____

Password Hint _____

PIN _____

Security Questions/Notes_____

_____

_____

_____

Name _____

Website _____

User Name _____

Password _____

Password Hint _____

PIN _____

Security Questions/Notes_____

_____

_____

_____

Starting with the Letter(s)

Name _____

Website _____

User Name _____

Password _____

Password Hint _____

PIN _____

Security Questions/Notes_____

_____

_____

_____

Name _____

Website _____

User Name _____

Password _____

Password Hint _____

PIN _____

Security Questions/Notes_____

_____

_____

_____

Starting with the Letter(s)

Name

Website

User Name

Password

Password Hint

PIN

Security Questions/Notes

Name

Website

User Name

Password

Password Hint

PIN

Security Questions/Notes

Starting with the Letter(s)

Name _____

Website _____

User Name _____

Password _____

Password Hint _____

PIN _____

Security Questions/Notes_____

_____

_____

_____

Name _____

Website _____

User Name _____

Password _____

Password Hint _____

PIN _____

Security Questions/Notes_____

_____

_____

_____

Name _____

Website _____

User Name _____

Password _____

Password Hint _____

PIN _____

Security Questions/Notes_____

_____

_____

_____

Name _____

Website _____

User Name _____

Password _____

Password Hint _____

PIN _____

Security Questions/Notes_____

_____

_____

_____

Starting with the Letter(s)

Name _____

Website _____

User Name _____

Password _____

Password Hint _____

PIN _____

Security Questions/Notes_____

_____

_____

_____

Name _____

Website _____

User Name _____

Password _____

Password Hint _____

PIN _____

Security Questions/Notes_____

_____

_____

_____

Starting with the Letter(s)

Name _____

Website _____

User Name _____

Password _____

Password Hint _____

PIN _____

Security Questions/Notes_____

_____

_____

_____

Name _____

Website _____

User Name _____

Password _____

Password Hint _____

PIN _____

Security Questions/Notes_____

_____

_____

_____

Starting with the Letter(s)

Name _____

Website _____

User Name _____

Password _____

Password Hint _____

PIN _____

Security Questions/Notes_____

_____

_____

_____

Name _____

Website _____

User Name _____

Password _____

Password Hint _____

PIN _____

Security Questions/Notes_____

_____

_____

_____

Starting with the Letter(s)

Name _____

Website _____

User Name _____

Password _____

Password Hint _____

PIN _____

Security Questions/Notes _____

_____

_____

_____

Name _____

Website _____

User Name _____

Password _____

Password Hint _____

PIN _____

Security Questions/Notes _____

_____

_____

_____

Starting with the Letter(s)

Name _____

Website _____

User Name _____

Password _____

Password Hint _____

PIN _____

Security Questions/Notes_____

_____

_____

_____

Name _____

Website _____

User Name _____

Password _____

Password Hint _____

PIN _____

Security Questions/Notes_____

_____

_____

_____

Starting with the Letter(s)

Name _____

Website _____

User Name _____

Password _____

Password Hint _____

PIN _____

Security Questions/Notes_____

_____

_____

_____

Name _____

Website _____

User Name _____

Password _____

Password Hint _____

PIN _____

Security Questions/Notes_____

_____

_____

_____

Starting with the Letter(s)

Name _____

Website _____

User Name _____

Password _____

Password Hint _____

PIN _____

Security Questions/Notes_____

_____

_____

_____

Name _____

Website _____

User Name _____

Password _____

Password Hint _____

PIN _____

Security Questions/Notes_____

_____

_____

_____

Starting with the Letter(s)

Name _____

Website _____

User Name _____

Password _____

Password Hint _____

PIN _____

Security Questions/Notes _____

_____

_____

_____

Name _____

Website _____

User Name _____

Password _____

Password Hint _____

PIN _____

Security Questions/Notes _____

_____

_____

_____

Starting with the Letter(s)

Name _____

Website _____

User Name _____

Password _____

Password Hint _____

PIN _____

Security Questions/Notes_____

_____

_____

_____

Name _____

Website _____

User Name _____

Password _____

Password Hint _____

PIN _____

Security Questions/Notes_____

_____

_____

_____

Starting with the Letter(s)

Name

Website

User Name

Password

Password Hint

PIN

Security Questions/Notes

Name

Website

User Name

Password

Password Hint

PIN

Security Questions/Notes

Starting with the Letter(s)

Name

Website

User Name

Password

Password Hint

PIN

Security Questions/Notes

Name

Website

User Name

Password

Password Hint

PIN

Security Questions/Notes

Starting with the Letter(s)

Name _____

Website _____

User Name _____

Password _____

Password Hint _____

PIN _____

Security Questions/Notes_____

_____

_____

_____

_____

Name _____

Website _____

User Name _____

Password _____

Password Hint _____

PIN _____

Security Questions/Notes_____

_____

_____

_____

Starting with the Letter(s)

Name _____

Website _____

User Name _____

Password _____

Password Hint _____

PIN _____

Security Questions/Notes_____

_____

_____

_____

Name _____

Website _____

User Name _____

Password _____

Password Hint _____

PIN _____

Security Questions/Notes_____

_____

_____

_____

Starting with the Letter(s)

Name _____

Website _____

User Name _____

Password _____

Password Hint _____

PIN _____

Security Questions/Notes_____

_____

_____

_____

Name _____

Website _____

User Name _____

Password _____

Password Hint _____

PIN _____

Security Questions/Notes_____

_____

_____

_____

Starting with the Letter(s)

Name _____

Website _____

User Name _____

Password _____

Password Hint _____

PIN _____

Security Questions/Notes_____

_____

_____

_____

Name _____

Website _____

User Name _____

Password _____

Password Hint _____

PIN _____

Security Questions/Notes_____

_____

_____

_____

Starting with the Letter(s)

Name

Website

User Name

Password

Password Hint

PIN

Security Questions/Notes

Name

Website

User Name

Password

Password Hint

PIN

Security Questions/Notes

Starting with the Letter(s)

Name _____

Website _____

User Name _____

Password _____

Password Hint _____

PIN _____

Security Questions/Notes_____

_____

_____

_____

_____

Name _____

Website _____

User Name _____

Password _____

Password Hint _____

PIN _____

Security Questions/Notes_____

_____

_____

_____

Name _____

Website _____

User Name _____

Password _____

Password Hint _____

PIN _____

Security Questions/Notes_____

_____

_____

_____

Name _____

Website _____

User Name _____

Password _____

Password Hint _____

PIN _____

Security Questions/Notes_____

_____

_____

_____

Starting with the Letter(s)

Name _____

Website _____

User Name _____

Password _____

Password Hint _____

PIN _____

Security Questions/Notes_____

_____

_____

_____

Name _____

Website _____

User Name _____

Password _____

Password Hint _____

PIN _____

Security Questions/Notes_____

_____

_____

_____

Starting with the Letter(s)

Name

Website

User Name

Password

Password Hint

PIN

Security Questions/Notes

Name

Website

User Name

Password

Password Hint

PIN

Security Questions/Notes

Starting with the Letter(s)

Name _____

Website _____

User Name _____

Password _____

Password Hint _____

PIN _____

Security Questions/Notes_____

_____

_____

_____

Name _____

Website _____

User Name _____

Password _____

Password Hint _____

PIN _____

Security Questions/Notes_____

_____

_____

_____

Starting with the Letter(s)

Name

Website

User Name

Password

Password Hint

PIN

Security Questions/Notes

Name

Website

User Name

Password

Password Hint

PIN

Security Questions/Notes

Starting with the Letter(s)

Name _____

Website _____

User Name _____

Password _____

Password Hint _____

PIN _____

Security Questions/Notes_____

_____

_____

_____

Name _____

Website _____

User Name _____

Password _____

Password Hint _____

PIN _____

Security Questions/Notes_____

_____

_____

_____

Starting with the Letter(s)

Name _____

Website _____

User Name _____

Password _____

Password Hint _____

PIN _____

Security Questions/Notes _____

_____

_____

_____

Name _____

Website _____

User Name _____

Password _____

Password Hint _____

PIN _____

Security Questions/Notes _____

_____

_____

_____

Starting with the Letter(s)

Name _____

Website _____

User Name _____

Password _____

Password Hint _____

PIN _____

Security Questions/Notes _____

_____

_____

_____

Name _____

Website _____

User Name _____

Password _____

Password Hint _____

PIN _____

Security Questions/Notes _____

_____

_____

_____

Name _____

Website _____

User Name _____

Password _____

Password Hint _____

PIN _____

Security Questions/Notes_____

_____

_____

_____

Name _____

Website _____

User Name _____

Password _____

Password Hint _____

PIN _____

Security Questions/Notes_____

_____

_____

_____

Starting with the Letter(s)

Name _____

Website _____

User Name _____

Password _____

Password Hint _____

PIN _____

Security Questions/Notes _____

_____

_____

_____

Name _____

Website _____

User Name _____

Password _____

Password Hint _____

PIN _____

Security Questions/Notes _____

_____

_____

_____

Starting with the Letter(s)

Name

Website

User Name

Password

Password Hint

PIN

Security Questions/Notes

Name

Website

User Name

Password

Password Hint

PIN

Security Questions/Notes

Starting with the Letter(s)

Name _____

Website _____

User Name _____

Password _____

Password Hint _____

PIN _____

Security Questions/Notes_____

_____

_____

_____

Name _____

Website _____

User Name _____

Password _____

Password Hint _____

PIN _____

Security Questions/Notes_____

_____

_____

_____

Starting with the Letter(s)

Name _____

Website _____

User Name _____

Password _____

Password Hint _____

PIN _____

Security Questions/Notes_____

_____

_____

_____

Name _____

Website _____

User Name _____

Password _____

Password Hint _____

PIN _____

Security Questions/Notes_____

_____

_____

_____

Starting with the Letter(s)

Name

Website

User Name

Password

Password Hint

PIN

Security Questions/Notes

Name

Website

User Name

Password

Password Hint

PIN

Security Questions/Notes

Starting with the Letter(s)

Name _____

Website _____

User Name _____

Password _____

Password Hint _____

PIN _____

Security Questions/Notes_____

_____

_____

_____

Name _____

Website _____

User Name _____

Password _____

Password Hint _____

PIN _____

Security Questions/Notes_____

_____

_____

_____

Starting with the Letter(s)

Name _____

Website _____

User Name _____

Password _____

Password Hint _____

PIN _____

Security Questions/Notes_____

_____

_____

_____

Name _____

Website _____

User Name _____

Password _____

Password Hint _____

PIN _____

Security Questions/Notes_____

_____

_____

_____

Starting with the Letter(s)

Name _____

Website _____

User Name _____

Password _____

Password Hint _____

PIN _____

Security Questions/Notes_____

_____

_____

_____

Name _____

Website _____

User Name _____

Password _____

Password Hint _____

PIN _____

Security Questions/Notes_____

_____

_____

_____

Starting with the Letter(s)

Name _____

Website _____

User Name _____

Password _____

Password Hint _____

PIN _____

Security Questions/Notes _____

_____

_____

_____

Name _____

Website _____

User Name _____

Password _____

Password Hint _____

PIN _____

Security Questions/Notes _____

_____

_____

_____

Starting with the Letter(s)

Name _____

Website _____

User Name _____

Password _____

Password Hint _____

PIN _____

Security Questions/Notes _____

_____

_____

_____

Name _____

Website _____

User Name _____

Password _____

Password Hint _____

PIN _____

Security Questions/Notes _____

_____

_____

_____

Starting with the Letter(s)

Name _____

Website _____

User Name _____

Password _____

Password Hint _____

PIN _____

Security Questions/Notes_____

_____

_____

_____

Name _____

Website _____

User Name _____

Password _____

Password Hint _____

PIN _____

Security Questions/Notes_____

_____

_____

_____

Starting with the Letter(s)

Name

Website

User Name

Password

Password Hint

PIN

Security Questions/Notes

_____

_____

_____

Name

Website

User Name

Password

Password Hint

PIN

Security Questions/Notes

_____

_____

_____

Starting with the Letter(s)

Name _____

Website _____

User Name _____

Password _____

Password Hint _____

PIN _____

Security Questions/Notes_____

_____

_____

_____

Name _____

Website _____

User Name _____

Password _____

Password Hint _____

PIN _____

Security Questions/Notes_____

_____

_____

_____

Starting with the Letter(s)

Name

Website

User Name

Password

Password Hint

PIN

Security Questions/Notes

Name

Website

User Name

Password

Password Hint

PIN

Security Questions/Notes

Starting with the Letter(s)

Name _____

Website _____

User Name _____

Password _____

Password Hint _____

PIN _____

Security Questions/Notes_____

_____

_____

_____

Name _____

Website _____

User Name _____

Password _____

Password Hint _____

PIN _____

Security Questions/Notes_____

_____

_____

_____

Starting with the Letter(s)

Name

Website

User Name

Password

Password Hint

PIN

Security Questions/Notes

Name

Website

User Name

Password

Password Hint

PIN

Security Questions/Notes

We hope you have enjoyed using "The Cup of Coffee."
Visit us at www.hiddeninplainviewbooks.com for
other resources you might enjoy.

Other titles in this series:
The Vault
The Maze
The Secret
The Cat
The Victor
The Dog

Please give us a fair and honest review on Amazon.
Your reviews help authors and product creators be
found by others who might enjoy similar offerings.

28132386R00066